Meditations
on the Trail

Meditations
on the Trail

A Guidebook for Self-Discovery

Christopher Ives

Wisdom

Wisdom Publications
199 Elm Street
Somerville, MA 02144 USA
wisdomexperience.org

Library of Congress Cataloging-in-Publication Data
Names: Ives, Christopher, 1954– author.
Title: Meditations on the trail: a guidebook for self-discovery / Christopher Ives.
Description: First. | Somerville: Wisdom Publications, 2021. |
    Includes bibliographical references.
Identifiers: LCCN 2020046561 (print) | LCCN 2020046562 (ebook) |
    ISBN 9781614297529 (paperback) | ISBN 9781614297680 (ebook)
Subjects: LCSH: Meditation.
Classification: LCC BL627 .I84 2021 (print) | LCC BL627 (ebook) |
    DDC 294.3/4435—dc23
LC record available at https://lccn.loc.gov/2020046561
LC ebook record available at https://lccn.loc.gov/2020046562

ISBN 978-1-61429-752-9   ebook ISBN 978-1-61429-768-0

25 24 23 22 21   5 4 3 2 1

Cover design by Marc Whitaker. Interior design by James D. Skatges.

Printed on acid-free paper that meets the guidelines for permanence and dura-
bility of the Production Guidelines for Book Longevity of the Council on Library Resources.

Printed in the United States of America.

Please visit fscus.org.

Contents

Preface

Each semester in my course on religious pilgrimages I ask my students what they think it means when someone says, "I'm spiritual, not religious." More often than not, they'll reply that being spiritual has to do with feeling connected to something larger than oneself, whether a higher power or nature. This often leads to a discussion of *how* connected to nature they feel, and more often than not they'll talk about how hard it is to feel connected when they're scurrying around in busy schedules and spending much of their waking time plugged into a device.

I don't think they're alone in feeling this way. Many of us, young and old, feel estranged from nature these days. Even if we don't suffer from what Richard Louv calls "nature-deficit disorder," we may see nature as separate from ourselves, "out there" as a place to which we go from time to time.

Of course, our feeling of disconnection from nature— from real nature, not shows on the Nature Channel—

is not caused solely by technology or our ways of using it. Many of us live in cities, in air-conditioned boxes, cut off from the sources of our food, ignorant of how our electricity was generated and natural gas extracted, oblivious of where our municipality gets water or where sewage goes when we flush the toilet. As a result, we lose our lived connection to nature and miss out on the health benefits that studies have shown are gained by spending time out in nature. This disconnection may even lead us to posit nature as an antagonist that we need to subdue and exploit. Psychiatrist Gerald May writes, "Feeling so divorced from the nature within and around us, we make wildness an adversary that we must tame rather than join, master rather than learn from."

Acknowledging this disconnection, let's pause and think about when we feel connected to the natural world.

What do you enjoy doing outside? Do you have a place in nature that, to you, is "sacred" in some sense? When do you feel most connected to nature?

Given that we are always animals in ecosystems and hence never physically disconnected from nature (even though we might be psychologically estranged), the real question is, "When and where do you most realize your embeddedness in nature?" Or, put more radically, "When and where do you most realize your embeddedness in nature *as* nature?" For me, it's when I'm hiking, or simply wandering in the woods. For others it might be while sitting outside in a favorite spot, gardening, kayaking, surfing, birding, or strolling through a city park.

I imagine that you, too, have felt a deeper connection to nature when you're outside and away from buildings and roads, especially when you're out for an extended time. As you've likely noticed, you don't need to make an effort to feel that connection. Simply spending an afternoon pulling weeds, a day walking along the seashore, a night reclining under the stars, a weekend camping in a national park, or a week clearing land can foster this sense of connection.

The feeling of closeness to nature can vary from person to person, of course. It may be a physical closeness, like when we are deep in the woods, surrounded by trees and rocks, or immersed in an activity, like gathering firewood, cutting brush, or walking along a path. It may be a sense of settling into our surroundings, like when we sit beside a stream or recline on a beach. Some of us feel close to nature when, like naturalists, we pay close attention to what's around us and notice particular things—a leaf floating down a brook, a lichen-covered boulder, a distinctive cloud passing overhead. The closeness may happen when our minds quiet down and we're filled with the beauty of a snowcapped mountain, a dazzling sunset, or a vast night sky. Others feel close to nature when they sense themselves as an animal in an ecosystem, entering into the food chain, interacting with other animals as kin, maybe even feeling awe and love for them.

Of course, sometimes when we're outside we don't feel connected to our surroundings. We may be lost in our heads, thinking or worrying about something back home. Or our activity may be infected by our ego, as we slip into hurrying, competing, reacting to others, trying to prove something.

At such times we can do certain things to plug in to our surroundings and be more fully there in the dirt, on the trail, under the stars. Maybe you have practices that you do when you're outdoors doing an activity you love. Maybe you say a word of gratitude each time you enter your favorite park, pause at the top of the mountain to take in the view before skiing down, or pick up a rock whenever you go out for a walk.

This book lays out an array of practices—some formal, some informal—that I have done over the years to deepen my own feeling of connection to the natural world, to help me realize how I am embedded in the vast, beautiful, and often intimidating system we call "nature." I mention several of these practices in *Zen on the Trail*, and that book can help put these practices in the larger context of, as the subtitle puts it, hiking as pilgrimage. As you will see, while the guided meditations in this book center on hiking, you can do most of them while engaged in any activity you enjoy doing outside, or simply while walking to a bus stop or sitting on a front stoop.

Many of these practices derive from Buddhism, especially the Zen strand of the tradition that I have practiced for nearly fifty years. I hope they can give you a taste of the states of mind and modes of experience that this religion sees as existentially liberating, at least as far as I understand them in my own limited way.

I also hope that these practices can support you in seeing your outings as more than a way to get good exercise or add to your list of accomplishments. Perhaps they can help you see your time outside as spiritual, however you define this term.

Doing these practices may even yield ethical fruits. A deeper sense of connection to nature around us, with an accompanying knowledge, love, and valuation of that nature, may be crucial to our waking up to climate disruption, feeling greater concern about what is happening to our planet, and taking action to mitigate the problem.

At the very least, I hope they will benefit you in some way—on the trail, back home, and across your life.

Acknowledgments

Like all publications, this book did not germinate and grow in a vacuum.

I thank my mother, Marilla, for letting me roam in the woods as a child, and my father, Bud, for introducing me to hiking over the many years he served as the scout-master in my hometown of Litchfield, Connecticut. I thank my brothers, Ned and Jeff, for making me feel safe on our youthful jaunts to "the river," down behind Forman School.

I thank my students at Stonehill College and participants in my programs at the Barre Center for Buddhist Studies for trusting me to guide them through these meditations out on the trail and giving me feedback about them over recent years.

I am also grateful to everyone at Wisdom Publications who brought this book to fruition: Josh Bartok for his editorial acumen, Ben Gleason for his skillful handling of the production process, Kat Davis for her adept marketing of the book, and Daniel Aitken for his wise leadership. I also thank James Skatges for the aesthetic sensibility with which he designed the book.

I dedicate this book to Mishy, who suggested compiling these guided meditations and has often practiced them with me, especially in the woods near Walden Pond during the pandemic. Her loving presence has helped me, at a challenging time, craft and refine what I am offering here.

Mindful Packing

Preparation is 80 percent.
—*Japanese saying*

HIKING AS A SPIRITUAL practice begins before we get to the trail. From the moment we decide to head out on a hike, we can start orchestrating the trip as a contemplative endeavor, not simply as a way to get some exercise or check something off our bucket list. One way to do this is to prepare and pack as a mindfully as possible.

The first of the seven principles of Leave No Trace backpacking is "Plan ahead and prepare." A big part of this principle is knowing the terrain and the weather we can expect to encounter and bringing what we need to stay comfortable and safe. We can start by reading a trail guide and taking a close look at a topographical map to get a sense of the route and the demands it might place on us. It's also worth noting the season and recent weather events where we'll be hiking; this can help us anticipate snowpack, ice, mud, and challenging stream crossings. The next step is to check the forecast for the place and imagine the weather we can expect along the trail, at different times through the day of the hike and at different elevations. In this way we can begin attuning ourselves to the place and responding skillfully to its conditions. The goal here is to accord with the place, not to muscle our way through it and endure conditions for which we are unprepared.

This is a first step to overcoming the dualism between me "in here" and nature "out there," for we are directing our attention to our anticipated surroundings and imagining how we will move in them, how we will function while fully embedded in a larger natural system and affected by all of its components, whether steep slopes, rushing water, driving rain, or piercing winds.

The next step is packing.

A few years ago I created a document with the ten essentials and the other things I might need when I head out for a hike. I modify it for other outings—whether a stroll in a state park, snowshoeing, cross-country skiing, or kayaking. By helping us remember what we may need out on the trail, a gear list can reduce mental agitation about whether we have forgotten something important.

When packing, try to not to see it as a mere practical task that ensures you have the right stuff. Instead, pack in a way that puts you in the right mindset before you set foot on the trail. To that end, pack slowly, perhaps while referring to a list of essentials. Appreciate the simplicity of having all you need—your home—in a pack. This is helpful for getting clear about what you need rather than what you want, which is, of course, the first step to simplifying your life in general.

After you have assembled, checked, and packed everything, step back and take a breath, in gratitude that you're now ready to head out to the trail. See if you can appreciate your filled pack as something organized, streamlined. Maybe even as a work of art.

By preparing this way, rather than simply grabbing some gear and throwing it into a pack, we can approach packing as a way to cultivate mindfulness. In the midst of the current mindfulness boom, people tend to define "mindfulness" as bare attention, attentiveness to what is happening in the moment, or awareness without judgment. The Pali term *sati* and its Sanskrit equivalent *smṛti* can be translated literally as "remembering," which is the meaning of the Japanese character (念) used to translate them. As we remember the things we need to pack, and recollect what we used on past outings, we are practicing mindfulness. And by slowing the process down and attending to each item, we are practicing mindfulness in the sense of calmly paying attention in the moment, free from our normal reactivity to what we experience.

When done this way, packing is an act of meditation. It is akin to a tea master slowly and carefully selecting the bowls, utensils, tea, and sweets they will use in the ceremony they are about to perform, harmonizing them with the seasons, tea house, and guests.

By slowing down the packing process, we can also enjoy our preparation for the hike as a meditative end in itself, rather than hurrying through it as a task that needs to be handled before we can get on the road. It can signal from the start that our intention is for the hike to be a spiritual experience, not some frenetic attempt to get a workout with the woods as our gym or do an "epic" to impress others.

By packing slowly and mindfully I also find myself appreciating each thing.

Some of the items—my water bottle, my trekking poles, my boots—are old friends, and I naturally want to thank them for roles they've played in past outings.

This gratitude makes me want to nurture them: to keep them clean and in good working condition, to repair them as needed, to get as much use as possible from them rather than replacing them when a new model comes on the market. This is what Zen folks refer to as *mono no shō o tsukusu*, to "make full use of the nature of things":

mending our possessions, and when they break down, finding other uses for them, like when we repurpose a tattered shirt as a rag.

We can also cull things we don't need. Depending on the hike and the weather, it may be the second water bottle, wool cap, polypro gloves, or rain pants. Reducing possessions to the minimum, simplifying, reducing weight—this practice parallels what an aspiring nun or monk does when she sets out to a monastery with only the few things she will be allowed to have. Like that acolyte, I depart for the trail with minimal possessions, emulating the simplicity of Zen monastic life.

Sometimes I do a similar practice with the contents of my briefcase, a desk drawer, and the glove compartment in my car (how many people actually keep gloves in there?), being mindful of what is in those spaces, culling things I don't need, nurturing whatever remains. This calm awareness (mindfulness) makes it easier to remember (also mindfulness) where my things are.

This is a good antidote to throwing things in bags and boxes, to making our living spaces chaotic and adding to our mental chaos.

In this respect, simplicity goes beyond having a refined, minimalist aesthetic and becomes a way to cultivate a calm mind. As an American monk says in a film I show my students about Buddhism in Sri Lanka, if you want to have a calm and empty mental room, you have to start by creating an empty physical room, or at least a room without clutter.

Pausing at the Gate

Dharma gates are innumerable,
I vow to learn them.
—*from the Fourfold Bodhisattva Vow*

How do you return the self back to
the mountains, rivers, and great earth?
—*Dōgen*

MOST RELIGIOUS SITES demarcate the transition from mundane to sacred space. Zen temples do this with a "mountain gate" (山門) through which one must pass to enter the compound. Shinto shrines deploy an orange *torii* gate, below which are troughs of water and bamboo ladles for washing one's mouth and hands. Catholic churches have a font of holy water outside the door into the sanctuary. These points of entry send the message that it's time to purify oneself of worldly concerns and enter a spiritual realm.

Such a threshold is something I value when I get out of my car at a trailhead.

With open time on the highway, my mind often fills itself with thoughts and worries. My nerves may be frazzled from traffic—or from the coffee I drank and the adrenaline seeping into my muscles in anticipation of the hike.

Perhaps you feel the same way when you get to the trailhead.

Try this.

. . . .

When you get out of the car, take a few breaths and do some stretching.

Move slower than usual as you put on your hiking boots, lock the car, stash your keys and wallet, and hoist your pack up onto your shoulders.

Do it mindfully, like a master serving a bowl of frothy green tea, or a martial artist demonstrating a dance-like kata.

Then find a threshold there on the edge of the woods, or, depending on your outing, the field, desert, or beach. It may be a trailhead information board.

Or two trees, a few feet apart near the beginning of the trail.

Maybe it's a break in a stone wall, or a bridge across a stream.

In that place of transition, pause, like monks and nuns do when they reach the mountain gate.

As you stand there quietly, note that you, like a monastic, are about to enter a separate space and time, a sacred realm of discovery. This is captured by the Japanese expression *nyūmon* (入門), "entering the gate," which connotes gaining foundational knowledge or skill.

Feel your body, ready and perhaps eager to start walking.

It might help to bend over and extend your fingers toward your toes.

Shake out any stress and tension.

You may even want to exhale loudly to expel any tightness in your body or gunk in your mind.

If any problems have been weighing on you, set them down here at the gate.

Tell them—and yourself—that you will deal with them after your hike, or at least the ones that merit getting picked up and taken back home.

Then take several deep breaths.

If you can, breathe from your *hara*, the area an inch below your navel that's your center of gravity. Extend your belly outward as you breathe in, and pull your belly in to exhale. This abdominal breathing will bring your awareness out of your head and down into your abdomen. It will help you calm "down."

To support this settling, as you exhale, expel whatever you've been carrying in your head: anything that has been worrying you, or something about which you've been obsessing. With each exhalation imagine this mental clutter flowing out of you, like exhaust coming out of a tailpipe.

Next, conjure up the intention to be fully in your body, in your senses, while on the trail today.

Plant a seed in your mind to remember to pay attention.

You may even want to come up with a phrase, like a mantra, such as, "On this hike I want to pay attention and be present," or, "Breathe, settle down, and be in this beautiful place." Or you can chant something longer, like the version of the Fourfold Bodhisattva Vow crafted by poets Gary Snyder, Philip Whalen, and Alan Ginsberg:

Sentient beings are numberless; I vow to save them.
Consuming desires are endless; I vow to stop them.
Dharma gates are countless; I vow to wake to them.
Nature's way is beautiful; I vow to become it.

Whatever it is, keep your mantra in mind throughout the hike. Or, at the very least, try to remember to pay attention, to be present and attentive to whatever you encounter.

Now, with your burdens set down and your intention focused, ask the forest, and all the critters in it, for permission to enter. You are entering their home, and you can do so with humility and respect, or, as Gary Snyder has put it, with good manners.

Next, under your breath perhaps, express thanks for the privilege of being able to go for a hike today.

With the woods open before you, put your palms together before your sternum and bow, reminding yourself that you're entering a special time and space with the intention to pay attention.

Then start walking, keeping your pace a notch slower than usual.

. . . .

With this practice at the gateway, we can cultivate mindfulness in its several senses: *remembering* that we are entering a special, if not sacred, time and space; intending to *pay attention* throughout the hike; and using a mantra of our own creation to *keep in mind* our commitment to hiking with calm awareness.

Through this ritual of pausing, breathing, bowing, remembering, and focusing intention and attention you may find that you have "collected" yourself. Here, too, we find a connection to mindfulness as remembering: recollection. Though you may have felt scattered as your monkey mind jumped around on the way to the trailhead, you have re-collected yourself here on the cusp of your hike.

At least that's the goal.

Easier said than done, of course!

Pausing in this way also reminds us that we are about to enter a complex place of beauty, and maybe even danger. We need to pay attention. We need to be attentive to the beauty of this place, and to its depths, antiquity, and beauty. We need to keep an eye out for spots on the trail where we can trip and fall.

Much of what will be happening around us we won't even begin to understand with our ordinary mind. So, like religious pilgrims, we need to maintain an attitude of humility, openness, and reverence, and in this way prime ourselves for experiences of awe and wonder.

Stopping at the gateway also helps me remember, as a non-native person, that I am in the homeland of the people who were here, in the case of Turtle Island/North America, since long before my ancestors invaded from Europe, and that I, too, am a colonial settler, a trespasser on native land. For millennia, indigenous people have lived in the region through which I will hike today. And they still do.

In my mind, I offer the indigenous peoples my gratitude and respect. I ask for their permission, too.

Now it's time to pass through gate and start walking, in humility, in gratitude, showing respect to those beings who dwell here.

Connecting through Your Senses

One time when he went to Mt. Lu, Dongpo awakened to the Way when he heard the voice of a stream cascading down a ravine in the night.

—*Dōgen*

The universe is composed of subjects to be communed with, not objects to be exploited. Everything has its own voice. . . . Thunder and lightning and stars and planets, flowers, birds, animals, trees—all these have voices, and they constitute a community of existence that is profoundly related.

—*Thomas Berry*

AFTER PASSING THROUGH the gate, entering the woods, and walking for a few minutes to warm up, I stop and check in with my senses.

Usually, as we move through the day or along the trail, we get lost in thinking if not worrying about things. Pausing and attending to what we're seeing, hearing, smelling, tasting, and feeling in our body helps us get out of our head and into what's happening around us.

It's an easy way to tune in to our surroundings.

It's also a good way to reinforce our intention to pay attention while on the hike.

Try this.

. . . .

Stand, or sit, with your arms at your side and your gaze falling onto the ground a few feet in front of you.

Shift your feet to stabilize your footing and balance.

Rest your awareness in your body standing there, filling a space in the woods,

Feel your boots contacting the ground. Note how gravity is directing your weight down onto your feet. Direct your attention to your leg muscles, keeping you upright.

Take a few abdominal breaths. Feel your belly extend outward as you inhale, and come back in as you exhale. As you inhale, breathe in fresh air, and imagine it entering your body.

While settling into this slow breathing, take note of what's been going on in your mind.

What have you been thinking about for the past few hours? Have you been entangled in any worries? Take a minute to monitor whatever is now arising in your mind. As you do this, you may get why Buddhists see ordinary consciousness as a sense organ and our thoughts as sense objects, too.

Now let's check in with your ears.

What sounds do you hear?

Any birds chirping? Is there a breeze rustling through the trees or over the rocks? Can you hear any cars in the distance?

Take a few minutes and track the sounds happening around you. Note how they arise, continue, then fade away.

Next, breathe in through your nose.

Smell the air.

What does this place smell like? Are there any odors you can detect? Fallen leaves? Muddy, musky ground? Pine sap? The fragrance of a flowering plant?

Now lick your lips and direct your attention to the taste in your mouth.

Can you taste anything distinct? The munchies you ate on the way to the trailhead? That last sip of coffee before you locked the car? The energy bar you gobbled before putting on your pack? What flavors can you detect?

Next, what are you seeing down on the ground?

Dirt? Rocks? Roots? Moss and lichen? Other plants? Any bugs? Take a mental inventory of what's there at your feet.

Now raise your gaze and look around you.

What's in your field of vision? As you scan, does anything catch your eye? Is anything moving?

Raise your gaze higher and look up.

What do you see above you? Are there any branches? Can you see the sky? What color is it? Are clouds passing overhead? Any distinct shapes?

Now, drop your gaze back down to the ground in front of you. Check in again with your five physical senses. Note the sensations of your body standing there. The sounds around you. The smell of the place. The taste in your mouth. The array of things you can see near your feet.

Take a breath and relax into this sense experience.

Let yourself be filled by the ever-shifting array of sensations. See if you can let go of being someone who has the sensations and simply be the sensations. This is a gateway to connecting with this place, to being filled by it, to dissolving any sense of separation from it.

Stay with this for a minute, filled with all the sensations, embedded in this place through your senses.

Now, bow to all that you've been experiencing, and resume your hike.

As you walk along the trail, see if you can stay in close touch with your sense experience. If you find at any point that you're getting lost in thought about something back home, stop walking and take a minute to tune in to the five senses. This will bring you back to your body and the woods.

Many of us are sight-dominant, relying on our vision while ignoring our hearing, touching, smelling, and tasting. When we talk about spirituality and waking up we tend to privilege seeing, as when we talk about "seeing into our nature" (*kenshō* 見性), seeing the light, getting enlightened, or having a beatific vision. While you hike, make an effort to focus on the other senses as well. Monitor sounds, attend to the smell of the place, and feel the breeze against your face, the roughness of the rock you clutch while scrambling up toward a summit, or the smoothness of the sapling you grab while descending a steep section of trail.

If you can, take your boots off when you stop for a break, and put your hot feet in a cold stream, or walk around barefoot to feel the ground on which you've been walking.

Simply put, embrace the place with all of your senses. Get intimate with it. You may even find that any sense of being "in here" apart from nature "out there" will dissolve, at least for a brief moment.

Expressed from a different angle, this practice of checking in with our senses can enhance our awareness of our embodiedness, not as a separate body covered in a layer of skin that demarcates the boundary between us and the world, but as a body that is always open to, connected with, and interacting with the larger nature of which it is part.

This *embodiedness* with vivid sensory experience is a valuable gateway to realizing our *embeddedness* in nature.

Moving at 80 Percent

It seems to have something to do with non-thinking, freedom from my usual figuring-out, strategizing, organizing, comprehending. My mind has simply quit such things. They just aren't happening. I don't remember ever feeling so free, but I don't care about that either. All I know is there's confidence in this moment, lightness inside and out. I have been slowed down. I have been slowed by a Power.

— *Gerald May*

LIKE WHEN PACKING gear, a skillful practice for hiking is to slow down.

So often in our lives we scurry about, multitasking, harried. It's unfortunate when we bring that freneticism along on a hike.

As an antidote, try doing each action at what feels like 80 percent of your normal pace.

At the end of class sessions I sometimes say to my students, "When you leave this room today, try walking at

80 percent of your ordinary speed as you head to your next class, the dining hall, your dorm, or maybe even the library."

As you hike, see if you can plant in your mind a mantra, a reminder: 80 percent.

Here's how you can cultivate this.

. . . .

When you are about to start walking, whether at a trailhead or outside your front door, pause for a second, take a deep breath, and say to yourself, "80 percent."

As you start to walk, reduce your speed by 20 percent. And while you're walking, keep "80 percent" in mind, as a practice of mindfulness.

You may find that after a while the words "80 percent" will float up in your mind on their own.

. . . .

You may discover that, by practicing in this way, something about your hiking will shift.

Over the course of your hike, you will likely stop hurrying.

You will feel more relaxed. You may even feel a calm spaciousness in your mind.

You may become better able notice things and savor their beauty: the hemlock seedling growing out of a crack in a glacial erratic, the jack-in-the-pulpit bowing to you as you pass, the music of a rivulet cascading across the trail.

Other benefits may accrue as well: Your muscles and stamina will hold up better. You will feel greater contentment at the end of the day. And your hike will be safer, for when you slow things down and pay more attention to the trail, you can avoid the stumbling and falling that can occur when we hurry. Fewer sprained ankles, fewer broken bones!

To promote this slowing and spaciousness, as you plan your outing, add on 20 percent more time than you think you will need to complete the loop, the out-and-back hike, or the up-and-down climb. This way you can give yourself more space—mentally and temporally—to savor all of the moments of the hike and make it all the more spiritually rewarding.

Back home, see if you can bring this practice into the rest of your life: move at 80 percent speed in all of your activities—talking, driving, cooking dinner, cleaning, walking to the bus stop.

You will likely discover that, as the day goes on, even though you've been slowing things down by 20 percent, you won't feel that activities are taking too long or you're falling behind.

You may actually feel that you're making better progress than usual, getting more done rather than less.

You may even find greater creativity and joy in your actions, especially those that might otherwise become rote and mindless, such as the "chores" through which we usually hurry.

Pouring Yourself
into Walking

When I asked my Zen teacher, Shunryu Suzuki Roshi, if he had any advice for working in the kitchen, he said, "When you wash the rice, *wash* the rice. When you cut the carrots, *cut* the carrots. When you stir the soup, *stir* the soup." Taking his words to heart, I found that they had the power to evoke what lies hidden in the depths of being. Something *awakens*. It is not self, not other, not me, not the world. To "be mindful while you work" carries a certain dryness, not to mention distraction: doing something—practicing mindfulness—besides what you are doing. What Suzuki Roshi meant was more like "*throw* yourself into it" or "*immerse* yourself in what you are doing."
—*Edward Espe Brown*

Pouring yourself into the Great Way of all the buddhas is how to extricate and presence yourself.
—*Dōgen*

THE GREAT JAPANESE Zen master Dōgen (1200–1253) advocated *gūjin* (究尽), which literally means "thoroughly and exhaustively" and refers to the act of pouring oneself into the activity at hand. Dōgen claimed that if in meditation you give yourself fully to breathing, you can let go of thinking, and settle down into calm presence.

Here is a way you can get a sense of this.

. . . .

Close your eyes.

Take a few breaths to get settled.

As you continue taking slow, deep breaths, think of a favorite activity to which you can give yourself completely and, in the process, free yourself from your troubles . . . at least for a few minutes.

Maybe it's dancing, playing a musical instrument, gardening, lifting weights, knitting, jogging.

Recall how you're able to pour yourself into that activity, with all of your attention and all of your body.

Imagining yourself doing the activity, and getting fully immersed in it.

Next, find a log or a rock on which you can sit comfortably.

If you're a meditator, get into your meditation position, at least as much as you can out there on the trail.

As you sit there, pour yourself into abdominal breathing. Gently push your belly out to breathe in, and pull your belly in to exhale.

To help you give yourself fully to breathing, try extending your outbreath a second or two longer than usual. Imagine every bit of air leaving the recesses of your lungs.

As you continue pouring yourself into breathing, notice when thinking arises and you lose your focus on the breath. When that happens, gently bring your attention back to your breathing.

And the next time it happens (and it will!), simply return to your breathing.

Meditation is less a dwelling in a state of tranquil bliss than a returning, again and again, to the simple act of breathing.

. . . .

This practice of immersing yourself in the activity at hand is not limited to formal seated meditation. Zen monks also do this when they practice walking meditation. They pour themselves into the activity of taking steps, feeling their body moving and settling into the rhythm of walking. We can hike in the same way.

Let's try something that will help us experience what this is like.

. . . .

Stand up straight, and lower your gaze onto the ground about three feet in front of you.

Start by taking short, slow steps.

Lift one foot.

Feel your heel rising.

Then feel your foot swinging forward, your heel landing, and your weight shifting onto that foot.

Do this for a few steps.

Now, with the next slow step, breathe in as your heel comes up and your foot swings forward, and breathe out as your heel lands and you place weight on that foot.

Do this with your other foot, breathing in as you lift it up and swing it forward, breathing out as you place it on the ground.

Adjust the speed of your stepping to get it in sync with your slow breathing.

As you walk, direct your attention to the sensations in your legs and feet.

Give yourself fully to breathing and walking.

Do this slow walking meditation for the next few minutes on the trail.

Next, try walking more quickly.

Gradually increase you pace over several minutes, until you're walking at your normal speed.

As you do this, don't try to coordinate your inhalations and exhalations with your steps. Just resume your normal pace, and keep your attention on your legs and the act of walking.

Then, after a minute or so, slow your pace down by 20 percent to make it easier to maintain your concentration on walking.

As you move along, keep giving your attention to the simple act of walking.

Just pour yourself into each step.

Really feel your heel hitting the ground, then the front of your foot dropping down and making contact.

Then feel your back foot lifting up off the ground and swinging forward. Feel each step. Feel your body moving through space, slowly, deliberately.

Just keep giving yourself to the simple act of walking.

Pour yourself into it.

Just walk!

After walking at 80 percent of your normal pace for a while, slow things back down again, and end this period of walking meditation by moving slowly like you did at the beginning.

Once again, connect each slow step to inhaling and exhaling as you swing your foot forward and set it down.

. . . .

This practice of *gūjin* connects to a core value in Zen: doing one thing at a time. In the tenth century, the

Chinese Zen master Yunmen supposedly admonished his disciples: "If you sit, just sit; if you walk, just walk—but don't wobble."

When out on the trail, take a break from multitasking.

Just walk.

Just sit.

Just swig from your water bottle.

Just devour the energy bar.

Doing Tasks as Meditation

Chop wood, carry water.
—*Zen saying*

IN ZEN MONASTIC life, *gūjin* extends beyond pouring oneself into breathing and walking. Monks and nuns also practice it when doing tasks that keep the monastery running, whether cooking, wiping down verandas with wet rags, or raking the gravel in rock gardens. When monks immerse themselves fully in this labor, it's called *samu* (作務).

. . . .

See if you can pour yourself into each of your tasks. Give your full attention to the packing process as way to cultivate calmness while arranging your gear.

Drive to the trailhead without multitasking.

After you park, immerse yourself in each action, doing one thing at a time, mindfully. Slow down as you put on your hiking books.

Attend closely as you insert your water bottle into the side pouch of your pack.

Notice how it feels to lock the car, and put your valuables in the top pouch.

Excitement is probably starting to flow through you in anticipation of hitting the trail, so if at any point you feel yourself hurrying through these actions, stop and take a breath.

. . . .

Once out on the trail, see each action as a chance to be fully in the moment, whether sipping water, eating a snack, filling your water bottle in a stream, adjusting the length of your trekking poles, or digging a hat out of your pack as you get above tree line. If backpacking, give your full attention to setting up your tent site for the night, like a tea master setting out necessary items and then performing a tea ceremony. As I wrote in *Zen on the Trail*,

> While at a campsite it's easy to follow the rhetoric of classical Zen and "chop wood, carry

water." We can do chores there as a kind of samu, work practice, fully attending to our labors as we pitch the tent, roll out the pad inside it, put the sheet or sleeping bag on top of the pad, and arrange the food, stove, and canister of propane. We get water from a stream, or gather snow to melt; we prepare and eat a meal. Just this.

In short, whether packing at home, driving to the trailhead, or moving along the trail, see each of the hike's activities as *samu*, as meditative acts, rather than as chores that you have to handle so you can on to the "good stuff"—the hiking itself, the berries along the trail, the dip beneath a waterfall, the buzz of topping out on a summit.

When you hike this way, you will likely find yourself calmer and more able to reside in the present moment, appreciating the little things, seeing more beauty, feeling more joy. Here, too, we find a gateway to liberation from entanglement in our reactive ego and its sense of being separate from the world.

Feeling Embodied

It is in this world,
with this body
that I sport ...
—*Ryōkan*

EVEN IF WE usually don't pay much attention to our bodies, hiking compels us to do so.

When stepping out of the car, we sense the air temperature and humidity (or lack thereof), feel warm or cool, and adjust our layers. As we pull on hiking boots, put a pack up on our backs, and take the first step beyond the trailhead, we're keenly aware of our energy level and aches. Then, as we walk along, we feel our quads swelling. We appreciate our arms as we brace ourselves with trekking poles or grab small saplings beside the trail. We feel the sweat flowing down our face. We realize that mosquitoes see our legs as sacks of blood. We get thirsty and hungry. We pee under the trees. We get sore.

One way to be more present on the trail is to embrace this physicality of hiking.

. . . .

Pause on the trail, then resume walking but at 80 percent of your normal pace.

Keep your breath slow and settled.

After a minute or two, direct your attention to your body.

Notice how you're breathing.

Is your respiration settled in your belly or fluttering in your chest? Is it fast or slow? Ragged or smooth?

Notice your physical temperature. Is there any part of your body feeling cold, or hot? Are you shivering? Sweating?

Feel your muscles working. Do they feel strong and energized? Is there any tightness or soreness in your body? Where?

Are you developing any hot spots on your feet? Do you feel any chafing on the inside of your thighs?

Now, continue walking for the next ten minutes.

While keeping your eye on the trail, feel yourself as an embodied being, in and as your body, moving along the trail. Feel your legs supporting your weight as you step forward, or up onto the next rock as you climb.

Notice how your arms are swinging at your sides, grabbing hold of rocks, or maneuvering your trekking poles to maintain your balance and take weight off your sore knees.

Feel the bulk and strength of your abdomen, with your pelvis and shoulders holding up your pack, and your lungs and heart powering your muscles as you move along the trail.

. . . .

This physicality of hiking mirrors the physicality of Zen practice and monastic life.

Back in the sixties when meditation was first becoming popular in the U.S., some people misconstrued it as an irresponsible escape from reality. Zen, however, sees normal human consciousness—with us lost in our heads, rehashing the past and worrying about the future—as having "escaped" from reality. Zen practice aims to bring us *back* to reality in all of its concrete immediacy.

This is promoted by the physicality of Zen practice, whether sitting on cushions or doing samu around the monastery. Zen literature is full of passages where, in response to questions about the essence of Buddhism, the master does such things as point to the tree in the garden or ask the questioner to go wash his bowls.

In a sense, Zen is about tuning in, not spacing out, being here, not going there. The path is to be in our bodies, in our senses, in this moment, in this place.

This is a passageway to feeling awe in the presence of an old-growth cedar; to standing in wonder of a rainbow in the mist around a waterfall; to seeing a meadow with dew drops on every blade of grass as enchanted.

Being an Animal
in the Woods

We can enjoy our humanity with its flashy brains and sexual buzz, its social cravings and stubborn tantrums, and take ourselves as no more and no less than another being of the Big Watershed.
— *Gary Snyder*

Walking is the exact balance of spirit and humility. Out walking, one notices where there is food. And there are firsthand true stories of "Your ass is somebody else's lunch"—a blunt way of saying interdependence, interconnection, "ecology," on the level where it counts, also a teaching of mindfulness and preparedness.
— *Gary Snyder*

SPENDING TIME ALONE at night in the backcountry is a good teacher.

As we sit by a fire or recline in a sleeping bag, we may hear a branch snap, a thump on the ground, some rustling in the bushes. Such sudden and unexpected sounds trigger a primal, animal vigilance in us. We look in the direction of the sound, squinting in an attempt to discern something out in the darkness. We scan around the tent site for the source—a bear, a raccoon, maybe another person. We listen carefully, wondering if we'll hear it again. We may clench our hands, and check to see if there is a rock or branch nearby that we can use as a weapon.

In these moments I really get that I'm an animal—just like the deer, bobcats, and crows. I'm a mammal, close kin to other apes and in the same branch of the tree of life as beavers and bats.

Like them, I'm out in the woods, eating, peeing, and pooping. I'm part of the food chain.

. . . .

Find a spot along the trail that calls you. Pause there.

Take a breath, and feel your body in that place.

Flex your quads in your upper legs. Feel your biceps. Open and close your hands. Make a fist.

See how you have opposable thumbs that can grab a branch as a club or a hammer as a tool.

Note how you have muscles that can serve you if you ever have to fight off another animal.

Now touch your teeth. Feel the points of your canine teeth.

Touch your hair on your head. Look at the hairs on your arms. This is your meagre fur, remnants of a time before humans had to make clothing to stay warm.

Feel your animal body there in the woods—is it cold? Warm? Hungry? Thirsty? Tired?

Are your animal senses on alert, monitoring what's around you?

Are you tracking sounds?

Are you turning your head abruptly when you hear a sudden noise or glimpse something moving in your peripheral vision?

Out here in the woods, do you feel any mild fear? Or intense fear?! Can you feel protective energy animating your muscles?

Other animals make distinctive chirps, yelps, howls, growls, and grunts: Dig down and investigate what animal sound is in you. What is your animal sound here in the woods? See if you can get in touch with that sound. And maybe even voice it!

Now, take a couple deep breaths.

Be silent for a minute.

Listen to the sounds around you.

Smell the air. Feel your body standing in this place, breathing.

Rest in this attentiveness for a few minutes, then bow out.

. . . .

Realizing that we are animals can enhance our awareness of being part of the beautiful and at times brutal realm of nature. Out in the backcountry we can feel the vulnerability and excitement of not being the apex predator. We can see ourselves as part of what Gary Snyder sees as a great potlatch of sharing and exchange as we eat and perhaps are eaten by other plants and animals.

Spending time out on the trail can also help us realize that the other animals in the woods may not be that different from us. Virtually all of them are sentient—they can feel pleasure and pain. They are aware, and, as far as we can tell, they can feel fear. They seem to have memories, and I assume they have purposes, however vague.

Traditional Buddhism sees them as fellow sentient beings, participating like us in the drama of rebirth and redeath. Tibetan Buddhists sometimes invite us to meet every animal we encounter with the awareness that it may have been your mother in a previous lifetime. Or it could be a deceased loved one now taking that form. At the very least we can see it as a kindred spirit, having consciousness and, like us, striving to flourish. Here, too, we can create a mantra as we walk. Maybe something like

"I'm a critter, too," or "I am walking through the home of other creatures."

By attending to how we are animals, we can start to overcome the feeling of separation from nature that is caused by our anthropocentric view that we are superior beings (a view shared by most strands of traditional Buddhism), living in our human societies apart from a supposedly dangerous realm of animals "red in tooth and claw," in which only the fittest survive. We can realize the violence in our own realm, with our wars making animal predation look harmless by comparison.

We may even find ourselves feeling safer walking through the wilderness than walking down the street.

Exchanging Air with Trees

Here is a tree older than the forest itself;
The years of its life defy reckoning.
Its roots have seen the upheavals of hill and valley,
Its leaves have known the changes of wind and frost.
—*Hanshan*

WHEN I HIKE, or simply go about my day, I tend to view the space around me as empty.

I take it to be a void through which I pass when I wander in the woods, walk into our condo, or drive down the road. I'm oblivious to the gases around me. Even when I feel the wind on my face I don't really get that what I'm sensing is gases hitting me. I know something is impacting me when a bug brushes against my forehead—but not when a breeze does.

Try this.

. . . .

On your hike, stop in a spot that strikes you as beautiful or comforting.

Take stock of the things around you—trees, bushes, flowers, boulders . . . whatever is there.

Feel them as fellow beings occupying space in the forest.

Now, scan your surroundings again, this time attending to the space between those objects.

Notice where there are volumes of open space around you, and how they wrap around the rocks and trees.

Take a few breaths, and feel how you're breathing in gases.

Though the air doesn't have much mass, each time you inhale you're pulling stuff inside you, like an eye-dropper sucking in liquid.

Recognize that what's out there beyond your nostrils is not an empty void but space filled with nitrogen, oxygen, carbon dioxide, argon, and methane.

Take a few breaths to savor these gases in our air.

Then ask yourself whether the air you're breathing has any smell.

Is it cool, or warm?

As you breathe in and fill your lungs, imagine the air

nurturing you, keeping you alive. (After all, without it you would pass out and die in a couple of minutes.)

See if you can conjure up some gratitude for this essential support of your existence, something we often take from granted.

. . . .

There's one other thing about which we're often oblivious. When we're on the trail or simply outside in a park, we may walk right past trees, barely aware of them, as if they were fence posts or telephone poles. (Granted, that may be their fate in the future.) But make no mistake, trees are living beings, too.

Though they can't walk or talk, they calmly do their thing—pulling water and nutrients from the soil; bringing it up through their roots, trunk, and branches; pulling in carbon dioxide from the air as they do photosynthesis; growing upward and outward. As scientists are now discovering, trees communicate and collaborate.

They do all of this quietly, without effort. They're unassuming, humble—no ego, no hype, no harming.

With these attributes they exude the kind of calm dignity to which we aspire. And some of them have been doing this—doing their thing in their suchness—for longer than I, or any person currently on the planet, has been alive.

As you stand there on the trail surrounded by trees, see if you can view them as fellow beings, supportive friends, elders.

Now, pick a tree that catches your eye.

Look at it carefully. How high up does it extend? Does it have leaves, or needles? What color are they? What is the bark like on the trunk?

What is distinctive about this tree? Its shape? Its roots extending across the trail? A broken branch? The angle at which it's growing? Some Spanish moss hanging from its limbs?

Next, as you breathe in, feel the air coming into your lungs.

Imagine the oxygen permeating your body.

Each time you inhale, imagine the oxygen coming out of the leaves or needles of the nearby trees and drifting to you.

Stay with this for a few minutes, taking in this offering from the trees around you.

Next, as you exhale, feel your breath passing out of you. Much of it is carbon dioxide. As you exhale, offer it to the trees. Do this for several breaths.

Now, when you breathe in, take in the oxygen from the trees, and feel it nurturing your body.

When you breathe out, send carbon dioxide to the trees.

Imagine the leaves taking in that carbon dioxide and then releasing oxygen back to you.

Keep doing this for a few minutes. Breathe the oxygen in, and the carbon dioxide out.

Settle into this awareness of your breathing as part of a larger cycle of gases, circulating here in these woods: through the trees, out into the air, into your body, back out of your body to the trees.

Feel yourself connected to the trees, dependent on them for oxygen.

Notice how in return the trees benefit from you, as you offer them carbon dioxide. Feel yourself in this dance of breathing and photosynthesis, in the complex system of relationships and processes that make up the forest and keep you alive.

Feel how you're part of this living forest.

Feel yourself embedded in nature.

· ·

Breathing is central to this and other practices here. Like the beating of our hearts, breathing happens multiple times each minute we're alive. This is probably the source of the connection between breathing, or respiration, and spirit. Both "respiration" and "spirit" derive from *spiritus*, a Latin word with both of these connotations. When ancient people encountered a corpse, they likely noticed immediately that the person's breathing had stopped, and together with this stoppage the personality and living energy of the person had disappeared. The spiritus of the person had left.

The primal, rhythmic activity of breathing oxygen from trees is not the only cycle in which we are embedded. Out on the trail we can direct our attention to the hydrological cycle: drinking water, peeing, offering salty water to the soil, and then water getting filtered out of your urine by the dirt, seeping into a stream, flowing into the ocean, then evaporating up into the air, riding atmospheric currents back to this region, falling as rain, draining into streams, being caught in our water bottles, getting drunk by us, then flowing out of our bodies again as we urinate and sweat.

When we are hiking, our sense experience, physical exertion, breathing, drinking, peeing—our embodiedness—help us realize our connection to our surroundings. Again, our embodiedness is a gateway to realizing our embeddedness in nature.

We realize this embeddedness in both senses of "realize": to become aware of and to actualize. That is to say, out on the trail we become vividly aware of our embeddedness and actualize it through our bodies when we breathe, walk, drink, sweat, spook other animals, and get spooked by them. And with the practices here, we can enhance this awareness of how we are interconnected with other events and processes in nature.

Though getting above the tree line or onto a summit can be a valuable goal, offering us stunning views or a sense of accomplishment, the deeper goal here is tapping in, not topping out. Strictly speaking, though, this not a matter of tapping into nature as something apart from us, for we are never disconnected from it.

We're always embedded in nature, even when living on the fortieth floor of an apartment building in New York.

It's just that we forget this fact of embeddedness.

Buddhism, however, encourages us to remember this fact, to attain insight into it.

Realizing Interbeing and Expressing Gratitude

When we look at a flower . . . we may think that it is different from "non-flower" things. But when we look more deeply, we see that everything in the cosmos is in that flower. Without all the non-flower elements—sunshine, clouds, earth, minerals, heat, rivers and consciousness—a flower cannot be.
—*Thich Nhat Hanh*

When we try to pick out anything by itself, we find it hitched to everything else in the Universe.
—*John Muir*

ALL OF US need a healthy sense of self.

We need self-confidence and self-respect. We need to feel empowered to pursue our goals. We need to maintain certain boundaries in the world and protect ourselves.

From the perspective of Zen, however, we can get trapped in the sense of being a separate entity and fail to see how we're woven into a larger system.

We can start recognizing and aligning with this interconnectedness before we even leave home. When heading out for a hike, give detailed information to a friend or family member about the trails you'll follow. Agree on a time by which you'll let them know you're okay. While creating a safety net when you're in the backcountry or up on a mountain, the sharing of this info will also acknowledge how your actions may affect other people, whether loved ones who might worry or the search-and-rescue volunteers who might have to set out in the night to look for you. It also shows respect by giving them the information they will need to come to your assistance effectively, without your loved ones having to wonder when to call the police or the rescuers having to search a broader area and with greater risk.

Once out on the trail, you can explore how you're embedded in nature as a vast system of interbeing.

. . . .

As you walk along, find a place that calls to you.
 Take off your pack and put it down. Find a spot to sit.
 As you settle into a comfortable position, sit up straight.
 Take a few deep breaths. Breathe in, drawing oxygen

into your body. Feel it nurturing you, keeping you alive. As you exhale, breath out any fatigue, pain, stress, or worries you might be carrying.

Just feel your body sitting there. Feel your butt contacting the rock, log, or ground. Feel the air sweeping across your face.

What are you hearing?

What do you smell?

What are you tasting in your mouth?

What are you seeing around you?

Now, as you sit there beside the trail, visualize all the things that have made it possible for you to enjoy this hike today.

First, there's the simple fact of your existence.

Think of your ancestors, who for thousands of years passed down your genetic inheritance. Think of all the processes that contributed to the existence of the sperm and egg that formed you. Think of all the nutrients during your nine months in your mother's womb. Think of all the people who have shaped you into the person you are, as someone who enjoys getting outside.

Next, visualize all of the inputs to the food you ate for breakfast—all of the natural processes, people, machines, and actions that contributed to your meal. Let's assume your breakfast included wheat in the form of a piece of toast.

Countless things and processes brought that piece of bread into being.

The sun: if it's shining right now, note its powerful presence there in the sky, and how it made it possible for the wheat to grow in Idaho.

The dirt on the farm: all the leaves, bits of wood, dust, nitrogen, phosphorous, bugs, worms, fungi, and microorganisms that created fertile soil.

Imagine clouds riding wind currents across the Pacific and dropping rain onto the fields.

And the farmer—her clothing, and the cotton that went into her clothes. The people growing and harvesting that cotton. The people working in the textile mill turning the cotton into clothes for the farmer.

Then there's the combine and other tools that the farmer uses. The iron ore deep in the earth, the miners who dug it up, the factory that shaped it into those tools. The gas and oil in the combine, and the countless organisms long ago who became the oil that someone recently drilled up from the ground. And then there are the engineers who built the oil well, the refinery, and the factory that produced the combine.

All of this and much more went into the toast that is fueling your muscles here on the trail.

Now imagine the natural processes happening where you are in the woods. The hydrological cycle of water moving through the region through which you are hiking.

The countless plants, animals, and geological processes that make up this place. The symbiosis between the fungi and the hemlocks, the wildflowers and the bees. And the people who made the trail. Those who maintain it each spring when blowdowns have to be cleared.

In your mind, or under your breath, say "thank you"—perhaps bringing your two palms together in front of your chest—in grateful acknowledgment to all of the people, animals, plants, sunlight, dirt, and water supporting you here. They've been making it possible for you to be out on the trail today and, now that you are out, they're contributing to the experience you're having—right now.

As you sit there in your spot, see if you can feel yourself in that web, receiving all of those inputs. Feel yourself embedded in a vast system of cause and effect, being shaped by countless other things and in turn affecting the world around you.

. . . .

Myriad things interacted for you to be born, to grow up, and to become interested in hiking. Countless factors came together to fuel you up at breakfast, transport you to the trailhead, make this trail, and create its surroundings. If we track all of the inputs and influences impacting us here in this moment, we can see that all of nature, all of reality, is contributing directly or indirectly to what is happening here on the trail. Expressed from another angle, in our being born, growing, breathing, eating, and walking we are woven into a web of relationships, and our boundaries are permeable.

Central to the path I am outlining in this book is release from our entrapment in the small self that feels separate from the world. I usually think, "I was born in 1954 and since then I've been doing my thing in the world, entering into relationships with other people and objects along the way," but it is more accurate to say, "Since 1954 the world has been doing its thing in and through the ever-changing configuration of energy that was labeled 'Christopher Avery Ives' by his parents." From the Buddhist view, relationships come first, individuals second, not the other way around. From the start we are inter-relational events, not separate entities who secondarily relate to other things.

The false sense of being an independent, enduring self/soul is accompanied by the subject-object mode of experience, in which we view things as objects completely apart from ourselves. Zen teaches that when we experience reality only in this way, we fail to realize how we actually exist: embedded in an inter-relational system, in an energy field. In the metaphor of waves and water, at one level each of us does exist as an individual wave with a temporary form, but insofar as we identify with and get attached to our formed existence as a wave, we are oblivious to the expanse of water—the ocean—of which we are part and of which we are an expression. We gaze nervously at the other waves "out there," unaware that we are all different facets of a whole. We feel cut off, alienated.

We also get afraid and defensive. We crave people, things, or situations that we think will make us safe, and we cling to the comforting things we already "have." All the while we react negatively to anything that threatens these objects of attachment. This results in the anxious, unsettled reactivity of like and dislike, attraction and aversion. In this way, we succumb to what Buddhism terms the "three poisons": *moha*, ignorance or delusion; *lobha*, desire, taking the form of craving and clinging; and *dosa*, dislike, ill will, anger, hatred.

In short, feeling cut off from the world as we experience things dualistically, and being filled with these three unhealthy mental states, we suffer.

One way to slip out of this ego that feels separate and is caught up in detrimental mental states is to realize a mode of experience in which we do not feel separate. This is what Zen is getting at with its notion of non-duality: not two and not one. We are not a separate entity (with a soul or unchanging essence) apart from objects of experience in the experiential mode of "twoness"; nor are we some sort of amorphous "oneness" like a mass of white light. We are neither a totally separate wave nor an unformed mass of water but an ocean-as-wave wave. In other words, "not two and not one," or non-duality. After waking up to this, we exist as ourselves, with our personalities and, yes, our quirks, while simultaneously having an awakened sense of being part of something larger.

Out on the trail, this is our realization of our embeddedness, our waking up in and *as* nature.

Settling into the Rhythm of Walking and Letting Go

I climb the road to Cold Mountain,
The road to Cold Mountain that never ends.
The valleys are long and strewn with stones;
The streams broad and banked with thick grass.
—*Hanshan*

OVER THE COURSE of human history, some renowned philosophers have done their thinking while walking. The German philosopher Immanuel Kant (1724–1804) went for a walk at the same time every day, so consistently that his neighbors reportedly set their clocks when he strolled past their windows. Kitarō Nishida (1870–1945), the most renowned Japanese philosopher of the twentieth century, would walk deep in thought from his home in northeastern Kyoto down to his office at Kyoto University, and his route is now a tourist attraction called the Philosophy Way (*Tetsugaku no michi*). This has made me wonder what it is that connects walking and thinking. But I'm more interested in how walking can help us *not* think, how wandering can help us calm and open up our minds.

Perhaps it has to do with the rhythm, like how drumming and dance can induce shamanic trances or simply get our minds off of our worries. Or how, in meditation, paying attention to the repetitive, rhythmic cycle of breathing settles our mind. As we've already seen, with walking meditation we can synchronize the rhythm of our breathing with the rhythm of our walking, at least at a slow speed.

I have found that rhythmic walking helps me early in a hike if I'm lost in thought or feeling resistance and late in the hike when I'm sore or depleted and reaching deep to cover the remaining miles back to the car.

Try this.

. . . .

Pause for a moment and take a few breaths to collect yourself.

If your legs are feeling sore or tight, do some stretching.

Next, focus your intention on keeping your legs moving and maintaining a steady pace and rhythm.

Start walking, and find a pace that you can maintain for a while.

As you walk at that pace, settle into a rhythm. Feel your legs swinging forward: right, left, right, left. You may even want to count your steps: one two three four, one two three four.

Pour yourself into the act of walking with a rhythm while counting your steps. Feel how this makes it easier to let go of whatever worries you brought onto the hike.

If you hit a steep section or need to scramble, adjust your pace but keep counting.

See if you can sustain this for five or ten minutes.

Then, when you stop walking this way, pause, take a few breaths, and savor the inner quiet now that you've stopped counting.

. . . .

This rhythmic counting-walking gives me momentum and takes my mind off of the thoughts in my head or the soreness in my knees.

Try it next time you're out on the trail and reaching deep to find focus and energy to keep moving forward.

Walking as Flow

Mountains are continually settled
and continually walking.
—*Dōgen*

ONE GOAL OF Buddhist meditation is gaining insight into impermanence.

A practitioner may monitor the ever-shifting process of thinking, contemplate bodily decline, meditate in a graveyard, or attend to the shifting of the seasons. In Zen, as we give ourselves to the breath and let go of thinking—or as Zen master Uchiyama Kōshō puts it, "open the hand of thought"—we can settle back into being part of a larger flow.

We can enhance our awareness of impermanence when we're out in nature, quiet and attentive. Sitting beside a stream, watching the water course by, and being filled with its gurgling sound is a passageway to entering the larger flow of which we are all part. We can also attend to the air moving around us, whether a slight breeze or howling wind.

Attunement to natural flow seems to have been what Zen teachers had in mind when they coined a term for novice monks: *unsui*, which literally means "clouds and water." Acolytes were being taught to attune themselves to shifts in and around themselves, and, in turn, to flow, from action to action, moment to moment.

Those of us who are physically active may find seated meditation a challenge, and it may be easier for us to intuit this flow when we're walking. Indeed, even without any formal contemplative practice, hikers report feeling part of the ever-shifting process that is happening around them: streams gurgling, birds chirping, clouds passing, trees growing, fiddlehead ferns rising up through the duff. They may even gain a sense of themselves flowing over—or together with—the landscape.

Try this.

. . . .

Stop at a place along the trail that calls to you. As you stand there, take a few breaths to begin collecting yourself and being more present.

Then, walk slowly for a few minutes to settle into walking.

When you start to feel immersed in the act of walking, start moving at a pace that feels comfortable and flowing.

You don't need to walk fast: flow happens with rushing streams and creeping lava alike.

As you walk, attend to how your legs and arms are moving back and forth and your body is constantly changing position.

Feel yourself gliding along the trail.

Notice how a part of your mind is tracking the surface of the trail and selecting spots on which to step, and how your conscious mind steps in and takes over when you have to scramble or find a way around a flooded section of trail.

As you continue giving yourself to the act of flowing down the path, imagine your heart pumping and blood coursing through your body. If hot, feel your body perspiring—releasing water from a body that is 70 percent water—to keep you from overheating.

Monitor how your sense experience is constantly changing, too, with different bodily sensations, different sounds, different smells, different sights, as you move along the trail.

See if you can feel yourself as a shifting configuration of physical energy.

Attend to how the air is moving around you, and trees and other plants are shifting shape, ever so slightly, as they grow. Perhaps there is a stream flowing nearby, too.

Use your imagination to see how the forest floor is shifting, as organic matter in the humus rots and bugs go about their business. Even rocks are eroding around you.

Then, allowing your attention to open up, feel yourself flowing over the landscape, with all the things around you flowing, too.

See if you can feel yourself as part of this interconnected, ever-changing flow, as part of the undulating energy field that is this place in the woods, inclusive of you.

. . . .

With this practice, as you let go of mental attachment and move lightly across the landscape, you may find yourself in a kind of "zone." Simply being the act of walking, without thinking about it, without thinking of anything, you may taste the "flow" that Mihaly Csikszentmihalyi outlined in his book *Flow*: full immersion in an activity, accompanied by feelings of joy and timelessness.

In this practice it is both your body and your mind that are flowing. We can flow when gliding along a flat and smooth section of trail or when picking our way across a talus field. Even if we shift from a steady rhythm to pausing and taking irregular steps, our mind can stay immersed in what we are doing. It can keep flowing along. The key is not to let the mind get stuck on something, for once it fixates on something other than our immediate actions, the flow stops.

Zen calls this the practice of non-abiding (*fujū* 不住).

Monitoring Thoughts

Most of the stuff that is going on in our mind is not about what is happening right here and now. Check it out sometime and see: most of the stuff that is going on in your mind is either chasing after the past or chasing after the future. Or worrying about the future and regretting or chewing over the past.

—*Blanche Hartman*

AS YOU GET flowing along in a rhythm or simply groaning and chugging up the trail, monitor your thoughts and feelings. See if they're flowing, too.

Try this simple practice.

Start walking, and after a minute or two, turn your attention to what's happening in your head—while also keeping your eyes on the trail!

Ask yourself some questions.

Am I daydreaming, imagining myself in some place other than this trail?

Am I obsessing about something?

Or worrying about something?

Have I been thinking about how far it will be to the summit, or how long it will be till I get back to the car?

Is there something I'm desiring, whether a soda, a slice of pizza, a shower, a foot massage, or a few more hours back in bed?

How am I feeling about this place? Am I drawn to my surroundings? Do I feel alien and intimidated? Are the rocks and roots, or a steep section of trail, pissing me off?

Notice how your thoughts rise up, shift as they flow across your mind, then disappear.

Notice when your thinking gets fixated on one thing.

Through the rhythm of breathing and walking, see if you can settle down into a quiet place from which you can observe these thoughts. Perhaps they're familiar, the ordinary denizens of your inner world.

You can view this mental activity as part of the "scenery of life."

Or, if they don't seem familiar, you can see them as curiosities.

On each hike, devote a chunk of time—five, ten minutes—to monitoring what's going on in your head. Observe how most thoughts shift and pass out of your mind, and certain thoughts stick around. Being aware of your thinking *when you're thinking* can help you get unstuck, out of your head, and back into the beauty of the woods and the joy of sauntering through nature.

Intuiting the Unborn

There is, monks, an unborn, unbecome, unmade,
unconditioned. If monks, if there were no unborn, unbecome,
unmade, unconditioned, no escape would be discerned
from what is born, become, made, conditioned.
—*Buddha*

The Unborn that I am talking about is the Buddha mind.
—*Bankei*

NEARLY FOUR BILLION years ago life emerged on this
planet. It evolved into humans, who passed on genetic
information across multiple generations, which got
included in a sperm and an egg that fused together. The
DNA mixed and molecules came together, till an embryo
formed as part of the belly of a woman, floating and
receiving nutrients from a tube. After several months a
brain formed, and then rudimentary sensation. At nine
months a baby emerged, and consciousness flowered.

From then on this ever-shifting being was nursed and nurtured, or in some cases harmed, until years later it became a fully formed human—you!

Unless we want to assume, like some religions do, that your essence or soul was injected by God into the egg the instant the sperm penetrated its wall, it seems impossible to pin down the exact point at which you came into being, the exact moment "you" arose as an individual with self-awareness and identity. In this sense, you are "unborn."

. . . .

After you have been outside for a few hours, find a spot to sit quietly.

Take several breaths to settle down in that spot.

Pay attention to the movement around you. Perhaps leaves are fluttering nearby in the breeze. Or clouds are drifting across the sky.

Then, as you sit there, attend to your thoughts as they float up in your mind, shift, and drift away. Feel your breathing as you exhale and inhale, exchanging carbon dioxide and oxygen with the trees around you. Feel your blood flowing through your arms and legs. Imagine your stomach breaking down breakfast and the nutrients getting carried through your bloodstream—yes, there's a stream inside you!—to the cells throughout your body.

Note how you're a configuration of inputs, a being who is embedded in a system of relationships, with permeable boundaries, just like the clouds. You are part of a grand process, emerging from within it and interacting with other parts of it.

See if you can recall the moment you came into existence. Though you might have a memory or two from infancy, I imagine you can't recall a distinct beginning. Like a wave moving across the surface of a vast ocean, there is no exact moment when you started. You are unborn.

For the next half hour, see if you can let go of your sense of being a separate thing with distinct moments of birth and death. Feel yourself as part of the larger process of nature, which has been flowing since long ago and will continue flowing into the infinite future.

. . . .

Practicing with the reality of being unborn is half of it. Also consider this: Down the line in our life, there will come a time when consciousness fades, breathing slows, the heart stops beating, consciousness lingers and then slips away, and the body starts decomposing, but what is the exact moment of dying, the exact moment we cease to exist? We can't pin it down, especially if we recognize that our mind-body is part of the larger process of nature.

We are undying, too.

If we can extend our awareness and self-identification beyond our body and our small mind, and gain insight into how we are part of a larger, processive whole, we can realize that we are unborn, and undying. This shift is spiritually liberating, for we are no longer construing ourselves as a separate, vulnerable entity that is going to die someday.

Extending Outward

As for me, I delight in the everyday Way,
Among mist-wrapped vines and rocky caves.
Here in the wilderness I am completely free,
With my friends, the white clouds, idling forever.
—*Hanshan*

ONE WAY TO complement seated meditation is to practice what I call "extending." Usually, we feel that we exist only inside our body, looking out at the world around us. Our minds pick things out, and we start thinking about them, perhaps labelling them, and responding with like or dislike. We feel that we are "here" and the things are "there." This dualistic mode of experience contributes to our sense of being a separate self, bounded by our skin. We can, however, expand our awareness beyond our normal sense of experiencing things from "in here."

Try this.

. . . .

Find a place along the trail that calls to you. Sit down, or stand relaxed with your arms at your sides. Take a few deep breaths to get settled.

Extend your gaze out as far as it will go. Take note of whatever's around you.

Pick something that attracts your attention on the far side of your field of vision. It might be a tree, a distant mountaintop, a cloud on the horizon.

Now, each time you exhale, as your breath leaves your body, imagine your awareness flowing out with it, and extending across the space in front of you, all the way to that object.

As you continue doing this, sense your awareness as something that extends beyond your head, beyond your normal thinking "up here" in your cranium. Feel yourself expanding beyond your body and the spot where you're standing. Feel your awareness "out there" with the object as it sways in the breeze or stands unmoving.

You may find that for a moment your sense of "having" the experience of the object will drop away and what remains is the raw experience, or, more exactly, just the thing, the event that is happening out across your field of vision.

For a split second it might simply be "balsam fir swaying in the breeze!" or "rocky summit!" with no sense of you in here having an experience of that thing over there. Just the experience. Just the thing. Just this. Just so.

Keep extending your awareness outward with your exhalations, and see if you can get a taste of this.

. . . .

Like other practices here, this extending outward frees us, at least temporarily, from our entrapment in the ego—our thinking, worrying, self-reflective consciousness—that feels separate from the world. It draws us out of identifying with the body bounded by our skin, or the consciousness residing in that body. It grants us a larger sense of self and helps us identify with something bigger than our ego or our body. On the trail, that bigger reality is the nature all around us. In all likelihood, getting a taste of this expansive awareness is one of the things that leads people to refer to their hiking as "spiritual."

Opening Up Sky Mind

As the Buddha instructs in the Majjhima Nikaya, "Develop a mind that is vast like space, where experiences both pleasant and unpleasant can appear and disappear without conflict, struggle, or harm. Rest in a mind like vast sky."
—*Jack Kornfield*

WHILE HIKING, LIKE in meditation, we may find that our busy mind quiets down. With fewer thoughts buzzing around in our heads, we start to feel calmer, and our awareness opens up. We may even get in touch with what has been inside of us all along, in the background: a quiet, open awareness, a calm spaciousness.

Buddhists often refer to this as sky mind. Thoughts, feelings, sounds, and other sense experiences drift through this spaciousness like clouds passing through the sky. We observe them and let them pass, without grabbing on to them.

Find a spot to stand or sit.

Put your tongue gently up against the roof of your mouth and take a few deep breaths through your nose (unless you're congested!). Feel your belly going outward as you inhale and coming in when you exhale.

Take a few minutes to check in with your hearing, smelling, and seeing. Get in touch with the sounds, smells, and sights in this place. Relax into the open field of sensations.

Feel yourself settling into this place.

Feel your awareness as a calm presence. Simply be present, witnessing what's happening around you.

Now, keeping your eyes open and your gaze extending out across your visual field, take a deep breath, and as you exhale, imagine your mind expanding outward.

This time, rather than extending your awareness to a specific object in your field of vision, imagine your awareness extending out across the entire landscape—across the woods, the slopes, the field, the desert, the beach, whatever the landscape is in which you find yourself.

Stay with this for a few breaths.

Now feel your mind opening upward, into the sky.

Imagine your mind as that vast open space above you. Feel yourself as a clear, quiet sky.

With this expansive awareness, take in what is happening around you. Perhaps you'll see a bird or a bug fly by and then disappear. Perhaps you'll notice clouds appear and pass by, eventually disappearing beyond the tree line or a distant ridge.

Now take a few minutes and attend to sounds in the space around you.

What sounds are you hearing? If it helps, close your eyes.

For a few minutes, keep your attention on the rising and falling of sounds, and note how they appear, and then disappear, in the expansive space that is your mind.

Next, observe any thoughts that might arise. When thoughts do happen, see if you can imagine them arising not in the cramped space of your little head, but in your larger sky mind.

Observe how thoughts float up, linger, and, if you let them go, drift away.

Notice when you grab on to a thought, and perhaps even run with it. Should you notice yourself rolling away in a train of thought, simply come back to your breathing, and pour yourself into the next inhalation and exhalation.

In this way, keep settling into calm, expansive awareness.

Feel yourself as an open spaciousness like the sky.

. . . .

In Japanese, the character for sky (空) also means "emptiness" and "space." This makes sense, for the sky is a vast and seemingly empty space. Likewise, our sky mind is an open, receptive mind. It's an inner depth from which we experience thoughts and external sense objects as they present themselves to us.

When we are in this mode of experience, we usually feel spacious, flowing, and free.

Getting Filled

From beyond past and present, mountains have been a great, sacred abode. Wise and holy people make mountains their inner sanctum, their body and mind. Through them, mountains have presenced themselves.

—*Dōgen*

We know clearly that the mind is mountains, rivers, and the earth; it's the sun, moon, and stars.

—*Dōgen*

OUT ON THE trail we may find that our mind opens up into a calm spaciousness. Viewed from another angle, as the mind quiets down, it's getting emptied. Zen often talks about meditation as a process of emptying. Sometimes this is referred to as "forgetting" oneself. Dōgen famously wrote,

To learn the Buddha Way is to learn the self,
to learn the self is to forget the self,
to forget the self is to be confirmed by all things.

What is Dōgen getting at here? How do we "forget the self"? What might it mean to be "confirmed" (証) by the myriad things we're experiencing out on the trail, or when walking down the street? If we look at what often happens to our minds when we're hiking, we can start getting a handle on this.

Try this.

· ·

Find a place to sit, and take a few breaths to get started.

As you settle there, look in front of you and select an object, whether a rock, plant, or tree trunk.

Sit quietly for a few minutes, being present to that object and experiencing it there in front of you.

Then, as you inhale, imagine breathing the object toward you, into your awareness. As you pull in air from around you, feel your awareness, your spacious mind, pulling the object toward you as well.

As you breathe it toward you, imagine your mind as an open space that encompasses that object.

Feel yourself as the spaciousness that envelopes it.

Notice how the object fills your mind as you breathe it toward you and embrace it.

Stay with this for a few minutes.

. . . .

As you may have discovered for yourself doing meditation or hiking, sometimes our mind gets emptied of narrative, and in turn we get filled by what we experience.

Maybe we've been looking down as we scramble up a steep and rocky section of trail and then lift our gaze . . . sunset! For a second, all that exists is the crimson sky. Our mind gets so filled by the gorgeous clouds that there no sense of a separate "me" who is *having* the experience. This can happen when we're at a concert and are engrossed in the music, so much so that there is no sense of me "over here" listening to the music "over there" coming to me from the musicians on stage. We might say that we were "filled" or "swept away" by the music, that it "washed over" us.

In these moments it is just the sunset, just the music.

Just this.

Just so.

Extending and Enveloping

Heaven and earth and I are of the same root;
the myriad things and I are of one substance.
—Sengzhao

WE CAN GET a different sense of who we are by extending our mind outward and enveloping what we experience. We can do this by linking these two practices to our inhalations and exhalations.

Try this.

. . . .

Choose an object out there in the woods. As you breathe in, feel yourself drawing the object toward you as your mind encompasses it.

As you exhale, extend your awareness out to the object.

Now expand your focus.

As you inhale, pull everything around you into your spacious mind.

As you exhale, feel your awareness expanding out across your visual field.

Breathe your surroundings in, and exhale your spacious awareness out across your surroundings.

Stay with this for ten or twenty minutes.

Practice resting in this place where there is no inside, no outside.

. . . .

It's just this—the vivid, vibratory reality that is happening here and now.

This, too, can give you a glimpse of the non-dual experience to which Zen practitioners aspire.

Presencing

Insentient beings preach the Dharma.
—*Dōgen*

The mountains and waters of the present
are the presencing spoken of by buddhas long ago.
—*Dōgen*

The true purpose is to see things as they are, to observe things as they are, and to let everything go as it is. . . . So concentrating is just an aid to help you realize "big mind," or the mind that is everything.
—*Shunryū Suzuki*

IN HIS "MOUNTAINS AND WATERS SUTRA," Dōgen tells us that "The mountains and waters of the present are the presencing spoken of by buddhas long ago" (而今

の山水は、古佛の道現成なり). What does he mean by this?

I think Dōgen is teaching us that when we "forget" ourselves, open up to what is happening around us, become fully present, and in this way "presence" ourselves, we realize how things present themselves to us, how they presence themselves.

This may sound obscure, but I think it's similar to what many of us experience on a hike. Needing to focus on roots and rocks along the trail, our attention shifts from thoughts to what is happening around us. No longer lost in our heads, we can be more present. We can "presence" ourselves as a receptive, spacious mind, what Zen also terms a mirror mind.

Once we presence ourselves in this way, we can receive each thing as it manifests itself in its exuberant flowering, leafing, gurgling, scatting, or chirping. That is to say, we experience it as it manifesting itself, as it does its presencing. In such moments, we get a clear appreciation of the thing in its vibratory presence. We receive it in its distinctiveness, its uniqueness, "just as it is," in what Buddhism terms its "suchness" (Skt. *tathātā*).

Let's see if we can get a sense of what this presencing is all about.

· ·

Pause at a comfortable spot along the trail.

Take a few breaths.

Relax and settle back into your mind as open space.

Look around and see what catches your eye—a fern, a flower, a branch, a tree trunk, a rock. Take a minute to find your thing.

Now, observe it closely—note its shape, color, texture, structure.

What is it?

Do you know the name that a botanist or geologist has given it? How is it existing here? Is it self-organizing, pulling nutrients from soil, light from sun, water from rain? Was it deposited here, whether by a glacier, a flood, or the wind?

Can you pick it up? How you might you transport it back to where you live?

What practical value might it have? How could you use it? Does it have monetary value? How much could you sell it for?

Now, step back and reflect on the thinking I just asked you to do with those questions. What I activated was your thinking mind. It's your discriminating, evaluating, calculating mind. Basically, it's our normal thinking.

Now, let's try a different approach.

Direct your attention back to the thing you selected. Let your attention fall gently on it.

As you breathe, simply be present to that thing before you.

When you breathe in, imagine it coming to you, filling your empty, open mind.

Do this for several breaths

Each time you inhale, in a gentle focus without thought, simply attend to how it's appearing to you in its distinctiveness, how it's presenting itself to you, just as it is.

Feel it as a vibrating presence.

Just sit there with its beauty, with the miracle of its existing right now and presenting itself to you in all of its simple glory.

Stay with this for a few minutes.

Now, as you continue breathing, feel yourself being present to that thing as it presents itself to you. Feel your calm presence receiving the presencing of the object.

Do this for several minutes, then bow to that thing, thanking it for its teachings.

· ·

Dōgen's term for this presencing is *genjō* (現成). We can attune to the presencing of things by being fully present. This is the presencing of ourselves as mirror mind or sky mind. When we are quietly present, we may find that self-consciousness and any sense of separateness drops away and what remains is "just this"—reality in its vital presence. In this moment the duality of the presencing of things and the presencing of self drops off, and what remains is the presencing of reality in its suchness. This is a moment of non-duality. The sense of a separate self that is the *subject* of experience *of* that *object* in the dualistic mode of experience has dropped off. This is Dōgen's notion of "forgetting the self," or, to use another of his expressions, the "dropping off of body and mind." We have no sense of being apart from reality. In a sense, we are not there, for what is there is simply *experience*, which, in that moment, is reality.

When, in our empty presencing, we are filled by the presencing of reality so fully that all that remains is *THIS*, we do not simply feel we are *part of* a larger system but that we *are* that system. In this way, we wake up to what Zen master Shunryū Suzuki called "the Big Mind that is everything." Here we can understand a possible origin of the pop expression, "become one with reality," or "become one with nature."

To use philosophical terms, *metaphysically* we exist in an interconnected energy field, a vast ocean in the form of myriad waves. Our practices of exchanging gases with trees and noting all the things that shape us can get us in touch with being a relational being that is embedded in a vast system. This insight helps us overcome the sense of being a fundamentally independent, autonomous entity, a separate wave. And in the practice of presencing, *existentially* we can wake up as the system itself, *as* the ocean, *as* nature.

With this approach in the background, Dōgen talks about the "unity of practice and confirmation [of Awakening]" (*shushō-ittō*)—the realization or *confirmation* of Awakening as the non-dual experience of the presencing of reality each time one in *practice* fully presences one-self by giving oneself fully to the act of breathing in meditation or to other ritualized activities around the monastery.

Here is where Buddhism is indeed a religion, a way to deal with finitude, with mortality. In presencing, in waking up to Big Mind, we extricate ourselves from the small mind, the little ego with its fear of death, and we gain a larger sense of self, extending beyond our mind and body. We identify with nature, with reality, something that is not born and does not die. Something that will continue long after our heart stops.

Simply put, the ordinary problem of what happens after death is not solved but *dissolved*. This opens up "salvation" as a *shift in identity* here and now, not as a *continuation of identity* in heaven in the hereafter.

Sitting Still and Taking In What's Happening

One moment, one encounter.
—*Tea ceremony saying*

SOMETIMES WHEN I'M out on the trail I find that meditative practices aren't doing much for me, or I don't feel like doing anything structured or formal. I just want to relax and enjoy my surroundings, without having to do anything. But I may still find myself thinking about things back home, or not being fully present to the woods.

In those moments, I'll simply stop, sit down, and quietly take in what's happening around me.

Here's what you can do.

. . . .

Remove your pack and find a place to sit down beside the trail.

Settle into breathing deeply and just sit there for a minute or so.

Then, start getting to know the place. Look around and see what's there. Are there any rocks or boulders? Any trees? What kinds?

What about other plants? Any moss, ferns, or wildflowers?

Or, if you're in the desert, what sort of hardy plants are growing around you?

What animals are doing their thing in this place? Do you see any bugs crawling on the ground? Flying around you? Blackflies? Mosquitoes? What about larger animals?

Can you see any birds? Do you hear any squirrels or marmots?

What else is happening? What is the light like? Is the sun hitting anything?

Is there any breeze? Can you hear any water flowing nearby?

What does the place smell like? How warm is it?

After using your senses to get a sense of the place, spend the next ten or twenty minutes tracking what's happening.

See of you can experience that spot as a center of activity, of organic and inorganic processes doing their thing.

And then, sit with the richness of your experience in that place.

Savor that spot and your encounter with it.

It's a unique encounter, never to be repeated.

After you get up and put your pack back on, take a deep breath, and stay with that spot for a few minutes.

Then, before you start hiking again, bow to it, and thank it for hosting you today.

. . . .

As we all know, some days we find ourselves outside with the same driven-ness that we bring to our work, studies, or other endeavors. We may feel amped up and antsy, wanting to click off the miles or hustle up the mountain, as if we're trying to work some nervous energy out of our system. Like busy days back in our ordinary lives, we may find ourselves doing, doing, doing. This practice of simply sitting in one spot and taking everything in, like many of the other practices in this book, can help us shift from frenetic *doing* to spirit-filled *being*.

By savoring that spot, we become more able to enjoy each moment of the hike, not just the peak experiences of topping out on a beautiful summit or checking another mountain off our list. The approach here is what Zen and tea masters are getting at with the idea of *ichigo ichi'e*. A direct translation of this expression is "one moment, one encounter," and it refers to appreciating each moment in its distinctiveness as something unrepeatable. Each encounter is indeed a once-in-a-lifetime experience—worth savoring.

With this attitude, we can join religious pilgrims in discovering that the journey, with all the unique moments along the way, offers rich rewards. And we can discern why it is that many religions talk about the spiritual path as one of return: by shifting from our normal scurrying—what some have termed the horizontal dimension of ego and doing—to simply being, and calming down into the vertical dimension of spirit, we may feel like we're returning home, to our source. As I sometimes remind myself when I succumb to nostalgia for some idyllic time in my past or for some lofty future attainment like Awakening, "It's always right here, right now, in the depths of my being."

With an emphasis on dwelling in calm *being* rather than frenetic *doing*, we can make our hikes restorative.

We can make them spiritually rewarding.

We can make them pilgrimages.

Extending Loving-Kindness

Whatever living beings there may be,
Whether they are weak or strong, omitting none,
The great or the mighty, medium, short or small,
The seen and the unseen,
Those living near and far away,
Those born and to-be-born—
May all beings be at ease!
—*Buddha*

A GOOD PRACTICE to make your hike a spiritual experience is to note spots of beauty or mystery that catch your eye and stir your heart. Maybe it's a flower blooming beside the trail, a small waterfall in the stream you're about to cross, a weathered snag sticking up above the young trees around it. Celebrate that thing by bowing to it. It doesn't need to be any big, dramatic bend toward the ground. A nod of your head, or a quiet "thank you," will suffice.

To connect with what's around me, I find it helpful to imagine the other animals in whose home I am walking. Like me, they are probably focused on getting through the day safely and securing water and food along the way. They, too (I assume), want to feel at ease, and to flourish in whatever ways that beetles, toads, foxes, and crows flourish.

When I go beyond simply imagining them and open my heart to them as fellow beings in this world of living and dying, I feel them as kindred spirits, even if I'm trying to ward them off with DEET or keep them away from my food.

Try this.

. . . .

As you hike, take note of the other sentient beings that are out in the woods with you. Are there any insects—butterflies, bees, dragonflies, beetles—flying around you or in the dirt at your feet? Do you hear any birds? Have you run into any other animals today—squirrels, marmots, rabbits, deer? Bears?! Do you know any other animals that likely inhabit this place?

Take a minute and feel them as your community of living beings along the trail.

Recognize their presence. Appreciate them as they do their thing in their forest or mountain home.

Then, extend love to them. Use whatever words ring true to you. What often bubbles up in my mind is "May you flourish, free from suffering." Or, as I recently found myself saying, "May all beings along this trail, my friends on the path, flourish together with me; and may this place flourish, too, unharmed by humans, in its beauty and biodiversity."

As you continue on your hike, whenever you encounter something striking that is presenting itself to you, pause, thank it, and wish it the best.

. . . .

In traditional Buddhism the practice of extending loving-kindness (Pali *mettā*; Skt. *maitrī*) aims to purify the mind of ill will, just as the practice of generous giving aims to purify the mind of greed. Extending loving-kindness while out on the trail can also help us feel a connection to other beings in the woods, whether animals or plants. Opening up our hearts to them, feeling gratitude for what they contribute through their niche in the ecosystem, and wishing them the best, we may discover a kinship with them, if not camaraderie.

They may even become what Buddhism terms "friends on the path" (Pali *kalyāṇa-mitta*).

We may see them as fellow members of our spiritual community, our sangha.

We can even form what Gary Snyder terms the Great Earth Sangha, in which humans and other animals "can accept each other as barefoot equals sleeping on the same ground."

Leaving No Trace

When you do something,
you should burn yourself completely,
like a good bonfire,
leaving no trace of yourself.
—*Shunryū Suzuki*

Since the great sages entered the mountains, no one has encountered them there. There is simply the presencing of the mountain activity, with no trace of their having entered.
—*Dōgen*

CENTRAL TO ETHICAL, low-impact hiking and backpacking are the seven principles of Leave No Trace:

1. Plan ahead and prepare.
2. Travel and camp on durable surfaces.
3. Dispose of waste properly.

4. Leave what you find.
5. Minimize campfire impacts.
6. Respect wildlife.
7. Be considerate of other visitors.

"Leaving no trace" (*museki*) is a core value in Zen, too. As the above statement by Shunryū Suzuki indicates, it has to do with fully engaging the task at hand, doing it completely and well, then letting go, unattached to what you have done or the praise you might get. As I wrote in *Zen on the Trail*, "Show up each moment with no investment in making your mark or trying to prove something, and with as much savvy and compassion as you can muster, just do what needs to be done. Then let go."

As a kind of meditation on the trail, we can practice Leave No Trace in these various senses.

. . . .

On your hike, see if you can walk along without leaving any sign that you were there.

Tread lightly.

Stay on the trail.

Depending on the terrain, avoid heavy hiking boots with hard soles that can contribute to erosion or harm plants.

Move quietly, without disturbing animals, as you walk through their home.

Make sure you don't drop any candy wrappers, or break the stems of delicate wildflowers, or leave circled rocks and a pile of ashes where you enjoyed a fire.

Better yet, don't make a fire.

And if you have to poop, dig a cat hole at least six inches deep, or, better yet, use a WAG bag to carry out your poop.

See if you can walk attentively, with an unobtrusive presence, observing what's around you. If you are with others, try not to yell, and avoid talking loudly when taking a break or hanging out at your tent site.

. . . .

Though some of this may seem like self-deprivation, holding back in this way can deepen our calm presencing, not to mention minimizing disturbance and reducing our ecological footprint on the places of beauty—often fragile—through which we walk.

Back in your ordinary life you can apply Leave No Trace to your activities—what you eat, what you wear, how you get places, what you do for recreation. As the first precept in Buddhism exhorts us, "Refrain from harming living beings." Ultimately, this harm is the trace we should avoid leaving, whether on the trail or on our longer pilgrimage through life.

Maybe this is our core practice: treading lightly on the trail, on all our paths, leaving no trace, or at least doing no damage.

Slowing Down on the Way Out

My stories speak often of a Presence I encountered in the wilderness—or perhaps more accurately One who sought me out and drew me there. I called this Presence "the Power of the Slowing"; it was this Power that seemed to beckon, guide, teach, heal, and show me very deeply who I am.
—*Gerald May*

TOWARD THE END of a hike, when I'm tired and sore, I sometimes get sloppy.

I start hurrying, exerting my will to tough it out and get back to the trailhead. I pay less attention to where I'm stepping and what's around me. I may even trip, stumble, or take a spill.

If you should ever find yourself hurrying and scattered, try doing this.

. . . .

As soon as you notice that you're getting weary and sloppy, stop.

Take a few breaths to collect your scattered self, to bring yourself back to mindful collectedness.

Notice how your mind, perhaps to avoid pain, drifted off into imaginative daydreaming about munchies in the car or the bathtub in your home.

Remind yourself that most climbing accidents happen on the way down, not on the ascent.

Take a moment to recognize what a blessing it is to be out in nature today, perhaps with loved ones.

Take another moment to feel gratitude for having the kind of body and health that make it possible to hit the trail or climb a mountain, and for the privilege, the luxury, of having time and resources to do so.

Feel your pain as a reminder of what you did today: getting out, exerting yourself on the trail, giving yourself vistas, camaraderie, enchantment.

Then, start walking again, but keep your pace at around 80 percent of your normal speed.

Direct your attention to what you're seeing and hearing around you.

Focus on the simple act of walking (pain and all) to the rhythm of taking steps and breathing.

Try counting your steps—one two three four one two three four—not unlike how in meditation people count their exhalations, one to ten and then over again.

. . . .

With this practice you can extend your mindful attentiveness and enjoyment across the entire hike, not just the pain-free beginning or the dramatic moments along the way. It will also help you make it back to the trailhead without getting hurt!

Concluding the Hike

The challenge is to learn how to carry over the quality of the journey into your everyday life.
— *Phil Cousineau*

WHEN WE COME to the end of hike, most of us are eager to escape our soreness and fatigue. Seeing asphalt and parked cars may come as a relief, for these constructions may signify that we are on the cusp of reclaiming our creature comforts.

Others of us may feel sadness, knowing that we are leaving the sanctuary that is the trail and about to re-engage the bustle of our lives. We may experience a tug to turn around and disappear back into the woods.

Either way, I find it helpful to bring closure to my hikes.

. . . .

When you get back to the trailhead, rather than hurrying to the food in the car or to the pleasure of sitting down and taking your boots off, pause at the gateway where you bowed at the beginning of the hike.

Turn around and face the woods.

Stand there in that threshold between the woods and the parking lot.

Take a few breaths and take stock of your experiences on the trail today.

Any highlights?

What blessings did you get from the hike?

What are the boons of today's pilgrimage into nature?

Did you experience something new? Learn something? Let go of something?

Express gratitude in your own way—it can be a bow, a prayer, some words of thanks.

Then head back to your car.

On the drive home, see if you can keep your phone in your pocket and just drive (or just ride as a passenger).

Through the rest of the day, try to stay with your breath. Pause and take three breaths when you feel that you are distracted or hurrying.

Do actions at 80 percent of your normal speed as a way to bridge the trail and your ordinary life, to maintain at least some of the mindful calm you might have felt in the woods.

See if you can integrate the practices in this book—and everything you experience while doing them on the trail—into your daily life, and ultimately into the master hike that is your lifelong journey here in this beautiful and complex world.

Appendix:
Seated Meditation

If you don't have a meditation technique already, here is how in *Zen on the Trail* I described doing Zen seated meditation—*zazen*—while out on a hike. Whether done outside or indoors in a more formal setting, this practice of seated meditation is foundational to the various practices I set forth above.

. . . .

Take off your pack. Find a flat rock about eight inches off the ground. Sit on the front edge, cross your legs comfortably, sit up straight. Touch the ground with your hand to fully contact that place, like the Buddha did when he touched the ground in the "earth-touching gesture" and proclaimed to Māra, "The earth is my witness." Feel that spot as your seat, your version of the place where the Buddha sat, his seat of diamond-sharp wisdom.

Put your right hand down on your lap, palm up. Then place your left hand, palm up, on top of the right, with thumb tips touching. In this position your hands will form a round cradle and be encompassed by your arms as a bigger circle, just like how you are contained in and part of the big circle of the universe.

Let your gaze drop down to a spot on the ground about eighteen inches in front of you. Feel yourself sitting there. A pyramid of flesh and bone, polypro and fleece. Aldo Leopold spoke of "thinking like a mountain," but on a hike try sitting like a mountain. Settle there. Sit with a broad, firm base. Imagine your butt sinking deep into the earth. Feel your chest as a cliff, your shoulders as spurs slanting off the summit cone. Feel the weathered ridge of your nose, and the summit on the top of your head. Feel the sun and breeze hitting your slopes. Feel the heat rising off your head. Feel your solidity as you sit there. Feel the aches and sweat.

Breathe in the woods around you. And if you can do it without effort, breathe abdominally, from what Japanese monks and martial artists call the *hara*, your center of gravity in the belly, about an inch below your navel. To inhale, gently push out your belly like a rotund Buddha sculpture in a garden, and bring it back in slowly to send the breath out. Feel your breath come in, bringing fresh air, full of oxygen that is being offered by the larches, cedars, and mountain laurel around you. Feel the air slowly leave through your nostrils. Extend your out-breath slightly until your lungs are empty. Offer up the carbon dioxide to the plants around you.

Then just continue to breathe. Pour yourself into each outbreath. Let sounds enter you, and pass through. Be fully there as a mountain.

After five, ten, or thirty minutes, place your palms together in front of your chest and bow.

When you start to move again, do one thing at a time. Slowly. Extend your legs. Stand up.

Remain still for a minute. Lift your pack and put it on. Latch the hip belt and sternum strap.

When you start walking again, slow your pace 20 percent. Keep it slow, with your breath at ease. And as you continue along the trail and through the day, keep doing just one thing at a time. Give yourself to each step. When wiping your forehead, just wipe your forehead. Just munch the trail mix. Just swig. "Don't wobble."

. . . .

Whether you follow these instructions or pursue another form of meditative contemplation, next time you do your practice outside, start by feeling the weight of your body on the ground. Feel where you're making contact. Feel the pressure on your butt, and possible sensations of warmth or cold. As you settle in your practice, see if you can feel your body pressing into the ground, like a mountain rooted in the ground. Feel yourself rooted, extending down into the firmness below you with no sense of difference between yourself and the earth beneath you. In this way, ground yourself, and feel the calm strength that emerges when we are "grounded."

Notes by Page Number

viii. *Feeling so divorced*: Gerald G. May, *The Wisdom of Wilderness: Experiencing the Healing Power of Nature* (New York: HarperOne, 2006), 65.

13. *One time when he went*: Ōkubo Dōshū, ed., *Shōbōgenzō* (Tokyo: Chikuma Shobō, 1971), 215. This statement appears in the "Keisei sanshoku" (The Voice of the Ravine, the Form of the Mountain) fascicle of Dōgen's *Shōbōgenzō*.

13. *The universe is composed*: Thomas Berry quoted in Derrick Jensen, *Listening to the Land: Conversations about Nature, Culture, and Eros* (White River Junction, VT: Chelsea Green Publishing, 2004), 36.

19. *It seems to have something to do*: May, *The Wisdom of Wilderness*, 16.

23. *When I asked*: Edward Espe Brown, "Leavening Spirit," *Tricycle: The Buddhist Review* (Fall 2002): 90.

23. *Pouring yourself*: Ōkubo Dōshū, *Shōbōgenzō*, 203. This statement appears in the "Zenki" (Total Functioning) fascicle of Dōgen's *Shōbōgenzō*.

30. *While at a campsite*: Christopher Ives, *Zen on the Trail: Hiking as Pilgrimage* (Boston: Wisdom Publications, 2018), 68.

33. *It is in this world*: John Stevens, trans., *Dewdrops on a Lotus Leaf: Zen Poems of Ryōkan* (Boston: Shambhala Publications, 1993), 50, adapted.

37. *We can enjoy our humanity*: Gary Snyder, *The Practice of the Wild* (Emeryville, CA: Shoemaker & Hoard, 1990), 25–26.

37. *Walking is*: Snyder, *The Practice of the Wild*, 19–20.

43. *Here is a tree*: Burton Watson, trans., "Cold Mountain Poems," in *Dharma Rain: Sources of Buddhist Environmentalism*, ed. Stephanie Kaza and Kenneth Kraft (Boston: Shambhala Publications, 2000), 55.

51. *When we look at a flower*: Thich Nhat Hanh, "The Sun My Heart," in *Dharma Rain*, 87.

51. *When we try to pick out*: John Muir, "My First Summer in the Sierra," in *Muir: Nature Writings* (New York: Library of America, 1997), 245.

59. *I climb the road*: Burton Watson, trans., "Cold Mountain Poems," in *Dharma Rain*, 54.

63. *Mountains are continually*: Ōkubo Dōshū, *Shōbō-*

genzō, 258. This statement appears in the "Sansui-kyō" (Mountains and Waters Sutra) fascicle of Dōgen's *Shōbōgenzō*.

69. *Most of the stuff*: Blanche Hartman, "The Life That Is Wonderful and Evanescent," in *A Beginner's Guide to Meditation: Practical Advice and Inspiration from Contemporary Buddhist Teachers*, ed. Rod Meade Sperry (Boston: Shambhala Publications, 2014), 111.

70. *scenery of life*: Kōshō Uchiyama, *Opening the Hand of Thought*, 86.

73. *There is, monks, an unborn*: Bhikkhu Bodhi, trans., *In the Buddha's Words: An Anthology of Discourses from the Pali Canon* (Boston: Wisdom Publications, 2005), 366.

73. *The Unborn that I am talking about*: Heinrich Dumoulin, *Zen Buddhism: A History*, vol. 2, *Japan* (New York: Macmillan Publishing, 1990), 317.

77. *As for me*: Burton Watson, trans., "Cold Mountain Poems," in *Dharma Rain*, 54.

81. *As the Buddha instructs*: Jack Kornfield, *Bringing Home the Dharma: Awakening Right Where You Are* (Boston: Shambhala Publications, 2011), 18.

85. *From beyond past and present*: Ōkubo Dōshū, *Shōbōgenzō* 265. This statement appears in the "Sansui-kyō" (Mountains and Waters Sutra) fascicle of Dōgen's *Shōbōgenzō*.

85. *We know clearly*: Ōkubo Dōshū, *Shōbōgenzō*, 44. This statement appears in the "Sokushin zebutsu" (This Very Mind Is the Buddha) fascicle of Dōgen's *Shōbōgenzō*.

89. *Heaven and earth*: Thomas Cleary, trans., *The Book of Serenity* (New York: Lindisfarne Press, 1990), 390.

91. *Insentient beings*: Ōkubo Dōshū, *Shōbōgenzō*, 397. This statement (*Mujō seppō*) is the title of one fascicle of Dōgen's *Shōbōgenzō*.

91. *The mountains and waters*: Ōkubo Dōshū, *Shōbōgenzō*, 258. This statement appears in the "Sansui-kyō" (Mountains and Waters Sutra) fascicle of Dōgen's *Shōbōgenzō*.

91. *The true purpose*: Shunryū Suzuki, *Zen Mind, Beginner's Mind* (New York: Weatherhill, 1998), 33.

101. *Whatever living beings*: "Karaniya Metta Sutta: The Buddha's Words on Loving-Kindness" (Sn 1.8), The Amaravati Sangha, trans., *Access to Insight (BCBS Edition)*, November 2, 2013, http://www. accesstoinsight.org/tipitaka/kn/snp/snp.1.08. amar.html.

104. *can accept each other*: Snyder, *The Practice of the Wild*, 26.

105. *When you do something*: Suzuki, *Zen Mind, Beginner's Mind*, 62.

105. *Since the great sages*: Ōkubo Dōshū, *Shōbōgenzō*,

265. This statement appears in the "Sansui-kyō" (Mountains and Waters Sutra) fascicle of Dōgen's *Shōbōgenzō*.

106. *Show up each moment*: Ives, *Zen on the Trail*, 53.

109. *My stories speak*: May, *The Wisdom of Wilderness*, xxiii.

113. *The challenge is*: Phil Cousineau, *The Art of Pilgrimage: A Seeker's Guide to Making Travel Sacred* (San Francisco: Conari Press, 1998), 227.

Bibliography

Bodhi, Bhikkhu, trans. *In the Buddha's Words: An Anthology of Discourses from the Pali Canon.* Somerville, MA: Wisdom Publications, 2005.

Brown, Edward Espe. "Leavening Spirit." *Tricycle: The Buddhist Review* (Fall 2002): 90–91.

Cleary, Thomas, trans. *The Book of Serenity.* New York: Lindisfarne Press, 1990.

Cousineau, Phil. *The Art of Pilgrimage: A Seeker's Guide to Making Travel Sacred.* San Francisco: Conari Press, 1998.

Dumoulin, Heinrich. *Zen Buddhism: A History.* Vol. 2, *Japan.* New York: Macmillan Publishing, 1990.

Hartman, Blanche. "The Life That Is Wonderful and Evanescent." In *A Beginner's Guide to Meditation: Practical Advice and Inspiration from Contemporary Buddhist Teachers*, edited by Rod Meade Sperry. Boston: Shambhala Publications, 2014.

Ives, Christopher. *Zen on the Trail: Hiking as Pilgrimage*. Boston: Wisdom Publications, 2018.

Jensen, Derrick. *Listening to the Land: Conversations about Nature, Culture, and Eros*. White River Junction, VT: Chelsea Green Publishing Company, 2004.

"Karaniya Metta Sutta: The Buddha's Words on Loving-Kindness" (Sn 1.8). The Amaravati Sangha, trans. *Access to Insight (BCBS Edition)*, November 2, 2013. http://www.accesstoinsight.org/tipitaka/kn/snp/snp.1.08.amar.html.

Kornfield, Jack. *Bringing Home the Dharma: Awakening Right Where You Are*. Boston: Shambhala Publications, 2011.

May, Gerald G. *The Wisdom of Wilderness: Experiencing the Healing Power of Nature*. New York: HarperOne, 2006.

Muir, John. *Muir: Nature Writings*. New York: Library of America, 1997.

Nhat Hanh, Thich. "The Sun My Heart." In *Dharma Rain: Sources of Buddhist Environmentalism*, edited by Stephanie Kaza and Kenneth Kraft. Boston: Shambhala Publications, 2000.

Ōkubo Dōshū, ed. *Shōbōgenzō*. Tokyo: Chikuma Shobō, 1971.

Snyder, Gary. *The Practice of the Wild*. Emeryville, CA: Shoemaker & Hoard, 1990.

Stevens, John, trans. *Dewdrops on a Lotus Leaf: Zen Poems of Ryōkan*. Boston: Shambhala Publications, 1993.

Suzuki, Shunryū. *Zen Mind, Beginner's Mind*. New York: Weatherhill, 1998.

Uchiyama Kōshō. *Opening the Hand of Thought: Approach to Zen*. New York: Penguin Arkana, 1993.

Watson, Burton, trans. "Cold Mountain Poems." In *Dharma Rain: Sources of Buddhist Environmentalism*, edited by Stephanie Kaza and Kenneth Kraft. Boston: Shambhala Publications, 2000.

Further Reading

Altschuler, Stephen. *The Mindful Hiker: On the Trail to Find the Path*. Camarillo, CA: DeVorrs and Company, 2004.

Coleman, Mark. *Awake in the Wild: Mindfulness in Nature as a Path of Self-Discovery*. Maui: Inner Ocean Publishing, 2006.

Dillard, Annie. *Pilgrim at Tinker Creek*. New York: HarperCollins, 2013.

Ives, Christopher. *Zen on the Trail: Hiking as Pilgrimage*. Somerville, MA: Wisdom Publications, 2018.

Kaza, Stephanie. *The Attentive Heart: Conversations with Trees*. New York: Fawcett Columbine, 1993.

Lane, Belden C. *Backpacking with the Saints: Wilderness Hiking as Spiritual Practice*. New York: Oxford University Press, 2015.

May, Gerald G. *The Wisdom of Wilderness: Experiencing the Healing Power of Nature*. New York: HarperCollins, 2006.

Mortali, Micah. *Rewilding: Meditations, Practices, and Skills for Awakening in Nature.* Boulder: Sounds True, 2019.

Williams, Florence. *The Nature Fix: Why Nature Makes Us Happier, Healthier, and More Creative.* New York: W. W. Norton, 2017.

About the Author

CHRISTOPHER IVES is professor of religious studies at Stonehill College. In his teaching and writing he focuses on ethics in Zen Buddhism and Buddhist approaches to nature and environmental issues. His publications include *Zen on the Trail: Hiking as Pilgrimage*; *Imperial-Way Zen: Ichikawa Hakugen's Critique and Lingering Questions for Buddhist Ethics*; *Zen Awakening and Society*; *Divine Emptiness and Historical Fullness*; a translation (with Abe Masao) of Nishida Kitarō's *An Inquiry into the Good*; and a translation (with Tokiwa Gishin) of Hisamatsu Shin'ichi's *Critical Sermons of the Zen Tradition*.

Son of a scoutmaster, he grew up hiking in the Berkshire Hills of Connecticut and Massachusetts. In college he started backpacking, and this passion has led him into the backcountry across North America and beyond. His outings in nature also include kayaking, bodyboarding, and open-water swimming. In addition to *doing* these activities, he devotes time to simply *being* in nature, whether meditating on the trail or sitting out on his back deck taking in the garden, trees, and sunsets.

What to Read Next from Wisdom Publications

Zen on the Trail
Hiking as Pilgrimage
Christopher Ives

"Like John Muir, Chris Ives knows that going out into the natural world is really going inward. This book about pilgrimage is itself a pilgrimage: we accompany the author as he leaves civilization behind to enter the wilderness and encounter his true nature and original face."—David R. Loy, author of *Money, Sex, War, Karma: Notes for a Buddhist Revolution*

The Poetry of Impermanence, Mindfulness, and Joy
John Brehm

"This collection would make a lovely gift for a poetry-loving or dharma-practicing friend, it could also serve as a wonderful gateway to either topic for the uninitiated."
—*Tricycle: The Buddhist Review*

One Hundred Days of Solitude
Losing My Self and Finding Grace on a Zen Retreat
Jane Dobisz

"An absolute pleasure for the soul."—Caroline Myss

Start Here, Start Now
A Short Guide to Mindfulness Meditation
Bhante Gunaratana

"A timeless, clear, and beautiful introduction."
—Tamara Levitt, head of mindfulness at Calm.com

Saying Yes to Life
(Even the Hard Parts)
Ezra Bayda with Josh Bartok
Foreword by Thomas Moore

"Astonishing."—*Spirituality & Health*

Landscapes of Wonder
Discovering Buddhist Dhamma in the World Around Us
Bhikkhu Nyanasobhano

". . . one of the most melodious new voices in Western
Buddhism to come along in some while."
—*Amazon.com*

Zen Meditation in Plain English
John Daishin Buksbazen
Foreword by Peter Matthiessen

"A fine introduction to Zen meditation practice,
grounded in tradition yet adapted to contemporary life."
—*Publishers Weekly*

About Wisdom Publications

Wisdom Publications is the leading publisher of classic and contemporary Buddhist books and practical works on mindfulness. To learn more about us or to explore our other books, please visit our website at wisdomexperience.org or contact us at the address below.

Wisdom Publications
199 Elm Street
Somerville, MA 02144 USA

We are a 501(c)(3) organization, and donations in support of our mission are tax deductible.

Wisdom Publications is affiliated with the Foundation for the Preservation of the Mahayana Tradition (FPMT).